Reconciliation Elegy

A JOURNAL OF COLLABORATION
PRESENTED BY E. A. CARMEAN, Jr.

ROBERT MOTHERWELL

WITH ROBERT BIGELOW
AND JOHN E. SCOFIELD

SKIRA
RIZZOLI
NEW YORK

Reconciliation
Elegy

© 1980 by Editions d'Art Albert Skira S.A., Geneva

Published in the United States of America in 1980 by

𝓡IZZOLI INTERNATIONAL PUBLICATIONS, INC.
712 Fifth Avenue/New York 10019

Library of Congress Catalog Card Number: 80-51574
ISBN: 0-8478-0337-6 clothbound
ISBN: 0-8478-0336-8 paperbound

PRINTED IN SWITZERLAND

On the title page:
Title of the painting written in charcoal
by Motherwell on the studio wall.

CONTENTS

Collaboration

E.A. CARMEAN, JR.

The photographic album and the comments by Robert Motherwell and his studio assistants presented here make up a journal which records both their collaboration in the creation of the artist's monumental painting *Reconciliation Elegy*, as well as how the painting itself was a collaboration between its intended placement—a commission for the National Gallery's East Building—and the artist's humanism. The story is simple and direct; but their common struggle to keep the great painting alive and personal is also complex and poignant.

Motherwell's studios in Greenwich, Connecticut. ▶

Fabrication

ROBERT BIGELOW

Now, I checked all the canvas suppliers in the city of New York, and couldn't find large enough canvas, a 12 feet in width canvas. Though the painting itself was to be 10 feet wide, we needed excess canvas, in order to stretch it around the wooden stretcher after the completion of the painting. So we needed at least a 12 feet wide canvas or thereabouts. The canvas we finally had fabricated to special order, and was approximately 12 feet wide and 40 feet long. It was manufactured far away, in the deep South of the U.S.A.

Canvas stretched on the studio floor.

Stretching clamp on the canvas.

ROBERT MOTHERWELL

I wanted the picture's surface not glossy, but matte. So I decided to size the canvas with gesso, rather than ordering the standard canvas-factory priming of oil paint. White-lead oil priming is not absorbent enough for what I was trying to realize. The pigment in gesso is plaster of Paris, and is as absorbent as white chalk, or paper, which makes paint more matte.

When I ordered the canvas, the canvas factory apparently didn't realize—because there were instructions *not* to prime it—that the canvas was going to be used for a painting. The canvas arrived folded in a package, deeply creased, like an unopened parachute. We were faced with the unexpected problem of getting the creases *out*. The canvas was so enormous there was no way to iron it, or anything else obvious. John Scofield, one of my assistants, invented an apparatus with which we could spread the huge canvas out on the studio floor and, with clamps attached to very long bolts, tighten the canvas every day. A month was spent tightening the raw canvas, in order to get the deep creases out. But this process had the unexpected advantage that we also got the "give" in the weaving out, so that when it was mounted on its wooden stretcher, the canvas didn't sag. (Primed oil canvas normally loosens through temperature changes by itself.) Step two was to "gesso" the big canvas, that is, to size it. Scofield and Bigelow put three layers of liquid gesso on it… A matte white, white as the houses in Mykonos, as alpine snow… intimacy and fear… my albino whale, as it lay there on the floor.

JOHN SCOFIELD

We painted this gesso ground onto the canvas, which was flat on the floor. We did it with brushes (rather than rollers) in order to work the gesso thoroughly in the fibers on the canvas. The first coat took quite some time because the raw canvas was very absorbent, and it took a lot of gesso. You actually had to do something you don't normally do when you are painting. We had to *jam the bristles* in between the threads of the virgin canvas.

Once the gesso was down, we didn't proceed any further with the next step for several weeks because, as we took this project in steps, anytime we completed a step, there would be a lot of discussion and a lot of investigating of various possibilities or various alternatives as to how to proceed from there. And so we took it a step at a time, very cautiously investigated every possibility, every option... After the ground was down, then we were ready to proceed with transferring the image from the very small original painted sketch. We'd already been discussing or working with the small original sketch weeks before, and we found that this original sketch was too small to square up accurately onto the large final canvas. It was just too vast a differentiation in scale. So what we did was have the small sketch blown up photographically to an intermediate size, at the Lithocraft Co., in Stamford, Connecticut. The working photo maquette for enlargement purposes measured 4 x 8 feet, and was on a sheet of utterly transparent plastic.

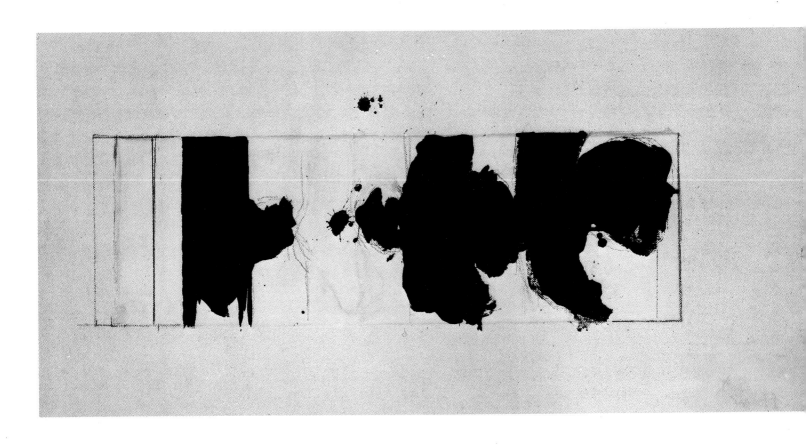

Ink sketch for Reconciliation Elegy.

ROBERT MOTHERWELL

We enlarged the sketch to about 8 feet long, so I could see more clearly the actual width of the pencil lines, the "feathering" of the painted edges, and so on. In effect, the photo maquette was serving the same purpose as looking at the original painted sketch through a magnifying glass. I wanted to be able to glance at it as I worked... the original painted sketch was much too small... Moreover the width of the *lines* was crucial to the emotional effect: in the original small sketch, the pencil lines were so fine that it was difficult visually to determine, say, whether one line was three times as wide as another more delicate line... In the photo maquette enlargement, I could tell almost exactly the differences in width. But when it actually came to make the large painting, I discovered I couldn't follow the photo maquette exactly. The thick lines if mathematically enlarged *in proportion* to the original small painted sketch became too powerful or too dominant in the large painting as I stood on it in my socks on the studio floor. But what if the true mathematical ratio was *necessary* from 100 feet? I realize now it was.

Photographic enlargement of Reconciliation Elegy *sketch with transparent grid overlay.*

Bigelow and Scofield transferring the cartoon.

ROBERT BIGELOW

All right, so we end up with a photo replica of the sketch roughly 4 x 8 feet. Then we drew up a grid of squares, which we superimposed over the photo image itself, which gave us guidelines to interpret the image onto the mural. Motherwell didn't want us to be *too precise,* just to draw him a rough "map" of about where he actually would be standing in the midst of the big canvas, brush in hand.

E.A. CARMEAN, JR.

In 1968 Motherwell spent long hours in the galleries of New York's Metropolitan Museum studying the works in the exhibition *The Great Age of Fresco: Giotto to Pontormo.* He had just begun his series of *Open* paintings, charcoal line drawing within a field of saturated color, and was thus especially taken by the *sinopia* panels of which the show mainly consisted—that is, under-

sections of murals showing the artist's original drawing for the fresco, done in the red earth pigment called "sinopia," in pure line.

That exhibition was recalled by Motherwell unconsciously in working out the problems of enlarging the black and white Elegy photo maquette. Indeed, when I saw the canvas on the floor in the Greenwich studio, covered only with white gesso, it had the feeling and the scale of an enormous, freshly plastered wall.

To translate the 16 inch painted sketch up to the scale of the 30 feet canvas, Motherwell combined two techniques used in the Renaissance for exactly the same purpose: enlarging by squaring an artist's final line drawing to mural–fresco-scale, but painting it spontaneously and freely, not slavishly, following the full-scale line drawing, the "cartoon."

ROBERT MOTHERWELL

The next step really goes back at least to the Italian Renaissance. We made what, in those times, was called a "cartoon," a rough "map" of the contours of the large forms, their placement. Since I had to paint the ultimate work while *walking on it,* inside its perimeters, most of the picture was out of the range of my peripheral vision. So we did rough guidelines, the "cartoon," a crude "map"… we did it by taking a sheet of paper, 40 feet long and 12 feet wide, and "squaring" it up, following the squares of the maquette photograph. We then drew in the outlines of the shapes with the new, final scale on this paper grid *over* the canvas. We had a little tool, traditionally used for centuries–a tiny wheel with spikes, like the kind you use to cut triangles of pizza; as we followed the lines on our paper over canvas with the little wheel, it made tiny holes through the paper onto the canvas. Then by rubbing the top of the paper with powdered Conté red chalk, the red chalk was forced through the paper to the canvas underneath, leaving a fine powdered hazy line. When the paper was finally taken away, very thin little lines, no wider than normal pencil lines, remained, outlining the big shapes. *My* map, my "cartoon," that I would energize...by painting with emotion, correcting by emotion... as the brush swept the canvas...or more exactly, through anxiety, through tension... otherwise the "cartoon" would remain impersonal, a mechanical blow-up.

SINOPIA. A large drawing on a wall made in preparation for painting a mural, which served as a guide to the artist for the general lines of his composition. It was done on the rough coat of plaster or arriccio, first in charcoal, then gone over sometimes in diluted ochre, and finally retraced in a red earth pigment called sinopia, because it came originally from Sinope, a town on the Black Sea. Its use was especially popular from the mid-thirteenth to the mid-fourteenth centuries, at the end of the sixteenth century, and during the early seventeenth century.

CARTON (in English usage, "cartoon"). The artist's final preparatory drawing of his composition, enlarged to the size of the wall area to be painted. The cartoon was laid against the wall over the final freshly laid plaster on which the painting was to be done. Its outlines were incised on the plaster through the heavy paper with a stylus. The resulting incised lines guided the artist in painting. This procedure was frequently used in the sixteenth century.

SPOLVERO (dusting or pouncing). A second method of transferring the artist's drawing onto the final plaster layer. After drawings as large as the frescoes themselves were made on paper, their outlines were pricked, and the whole paper was cut into pieces the size of each day's work. After the day's section of *intonaco* was laid, the corresponding drawing was placed over it and "dusted" with a cloth sack filled with charcoal powder, which passed through the tiny punctured holes, leaving an outline of the design on the fresh *intonaco*. This method was most popular in the second half of the fifteenth century.

From *The Great Age of Fresco: Giotto to Pontormo*

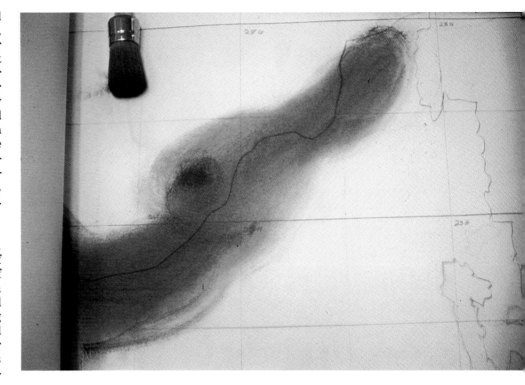

JOHN SCOFIELD

Every so often Bigelow and I would accumulate studio errands for Robert Motherwell that we ought to do in New York City, and we'd let them pile up to a full day's worth. One day, when the mural was at the point where the cartoon image was on the canvas (in red chalk), and Motherwell was looking at it and formulating in his own mind how he was going to bring it into being, Bigelow and I went in to New York City and did this trip. The last thing on the list of chores to do was pick up as many kinds of brushes as we could, specifically for this painting project. We came back to Greenwich with a big plastic bag full of every kind of brush you can think of, and laid them all out on the floor next to the painting. Well, next morning, Motherwell came down to the studio and looked at them; he tested the flexibility, the bristle, the shapes of the handles, and he instinctively knew which ones he liked and selected a few out of this stack we had brought back. So then I went to work in the machine shop, refitting meter-long handles that he liked onto the type of bristle-head he liked, which had been purchased with very short handles—they are only manufactured short.

Scofield refitting brush handles.

18

ROBERT MOTHERWELL

I realized that I could see a larger area of the canvas if my brushes had very long handles, at least 3 feet or 4 feet long, maybe more. So that, given the length of my arm... you see, my arm is a meter or whatever, then add another meter for the brush-handle, and the brush bristles became about 7 feet away from my shoulder... I was able to see farther, that is, see more *at once* of what I was doing. But also the long-handled brushes were crucial in regard to "the spontaneous"... If I'd used a short normal brush, my eye would have been so close to the surface that it would have been impossible to have that swept feeling of *largesse* that I wanted... nothing small-minded... petit bourgeois... nor finicky... but not pretentious, either... unrhetorical humanism... unmoved by establishment authoritarianism... indifferent...just *there*: A voice listened to or not.

Motherwell studying the original sketch. ▶
The photographic enlargement is below.

Motherwell's paint bucket.

Execution

ROBERT MOTHERWELL

The final step was for me actually to paint... I partly disregarded the red chalk lines. I didn't just *fill them in,* but *redrew them*... in charcoal... with my own emotion... the shapes slowly developed exactly as I had wanted them. The actual painting didn't take long... less than two weeks, all told... But nine months from the original sketch through all the various stages... (And three years to conceive that original sketch)... The difficult thing was psychological, *not to hesitate or equivocate.* I mean, having decided on the battle-plan, relentlessly to follow it through. At the end of a certain step, the work doesn't look like much; your whole impulse is to abandon the original step-by-step battle-plan, and to make it look complete at each stage. The hardest thing was to keep *faith,* faith that if I followed each step from beginning to end as planned, in the end it would come all together and at the same time would remain alive–not a mechanical enlargement. That discipline of faith I mainly followed... if I'd interrupted it at a certain moment, I could have lost the whole methodology... and with that, the sensation of "spontaneity" on a giant's scale. Patience! Faith! Self-discipline for an Aquarian, changeable as open air... (I did have a pitiful practical alternative: there was a second canvas ready, but "sized" from the factory with oil white lead... in case the first one didn't sing, for whatever reason.)...

One tries to foresee... but only God can be sure... And we were working to a given date, a deadline, for a specific architectural situation. Perhaps I should have refused an absolute deadline. A work is finished when it is finished, not by the calendar.

ROBERT BIGELOW

Before Motherwell started the mural, he spent several weeks planning his attack, how to approach the mural, how to execute it, he agonized over all the details of the execution. Then finally the day came that he'd really hashed over this thing and considered every alternative and was ready to go. And so he came down to the studio at his usual time, around 10:30, in his painting clothes, and was ready to begin. I remember at that time mixing up a bucket of about a liter of acrylic paint, mixing two parts acrylic Mars-black to one part water so that it was thin enough: it flowed freely. He likes it so that when he works directly with a brush it flows, it splashes, it has a kind of fluidity to it. Then he started with the charcoal and started laying in charcoal lines, figuring that he would work right across the mural in charcoal, and then come back and begin painting. Once he got into it, really engrossed in the execution of the mural, he immediately dropped that sequence and reached for the bucket of paint and started painting the left end of the mural.

Motherwell begins drawing in charcoal.

ROBERT MOTHERWELL

I remember that when I first started the actual painting, my heart pounded so hard that I could feel my torso literally shaking... (I have had a chronic irregular heartbeat for the last ten years from decades of earlier dissipation.) A couple of times I had to sit, just let my heart slow down. But when I mastered the painted image on the left... in a way, a picture in itself (I had begun from left to right for no particular reason), when the left image was finished, then I had some confidence... my heart stopped pounding. I went on painting, resting when my breathing came too fast from emotion and exertion. The brush was as long and heavy as a wet mop. I felt like a sailor mopping a ship's deck under a black starry sky... calm anxiety, anxious solitude. The canvas was so *big* underfoot, and beginning to stir, like a white whale.

Motherwell begins painting in black. ▶

26

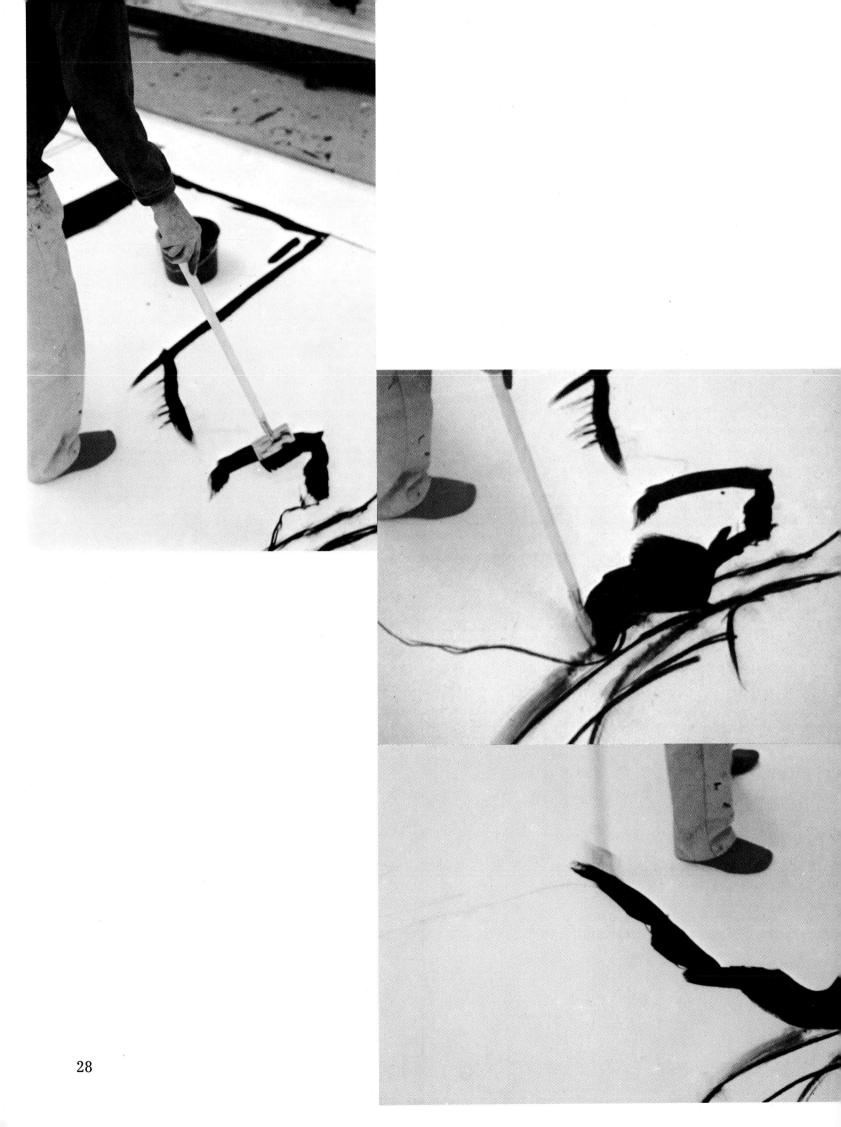

ROBERT BIGELOW

So the composition was set, the structure of the image was set, and he didn't have to work with "this", consider "this", or deal with "this", or manage "that" aspect of the painting. Now that was all done, that was all resolved, and it was just the execution; it was the direct, spontaneous, sensuous application of paint. At certain points, he had a white bucket of paint and he had a brush in the white and also a brush in black, and, at various times, he'd work some white paint into the black, and, with the edge of the black, back into the white, to create a kind of softer, ambiguous edge, and to integrate at times the background with the image as well.

40

ROBERT MOTHERWELL

Since we were using powdered red chalk, some of the powdered red chalk remained like red dust on the surface of the canvas. It suddenly occurred to me that, if I worked some of the chalk into the white paint, I could enrich and nuance the white. It would still "read" as pure white from a distance, but close-up, the brush strokes would be emphasized, subtly... the same thing with the charcoal. When you draw with thick charcoal, it's with burned wooden sticks... instead of blowing the black dust away, I went along the edge of the forms and picked up some of the charcoal dust with the wet brush. I was able to have modulations of Conté red *and* charcoal black in my white. (A danger of abstract art is to look too much like a poster or a rug.) The chalk and charcoal dust allowed me the "touch" of the painter's hand, that hand about which Henri Focillon has written movingly.

I became so absorbed that, though I wanted the painting process photographically documented, I asked my two assistants to leave. And then all went much more rapidly... how shall I say?... in the end, it is better to sacrifice total documentation for that focussed intensity that one can only feel when wholly alone. One tries to ignore social surroundings, companions, presences, but it's not possible. One has to feel only one's own presence. One's private vision, unsocialized and absolute. I do not live with a tribe, as earlier artists did.

44

*Photo turned on its side purposely to show the only view
the artist could have of its vertical appearance.*

*Motherwell studying the painting
with the working model opposite.*

ROBERT BIGELOW

Later he realized that the heavy chalk line that goes completely around the image and which acts as the "border" was executed insensitively, it was too heavy-handed all the way around, and it cramped the total image. So he went back with a rag, and rubbed those charcoal lines out, and worked them back in very lightly and thinly in places, and in other areas painted them out, drawing some of the red chalk line into the black chalk line, generally softening it, subtle tones between the red chalk and black chalk painted into the white. So he created a very sensuous, very sensitive coloration around the perimeter and into the background.

Motherwell signing the painting. ▶

JOHN SCOFIELD

Then came the moment when it was finished, and Motherwell was signing it. As he did so, he looked at Bigelow and me and said: "Your names should be here too."

Presentation

ROBERT MOTHERWELL

A painting has to be varnished to be protected… against fingerprints and scratches, against *air*. Everybody knows nowadays that the atmosphere is the enemy of any object, that everything is slowly oxidizing. Varnishing is a clear, transparent veil between the object and air. But the whole conception of this painting was to be extremely matte. (In fact, my preferred of all mediums in painting is oil paint on rag paper. Which is why I choose gesso, which is absorbent, like paper.) But gesso, being essentially white plaster, is extremely vulnerable to being spoiled. The difficulty with varnishes is that they are shiny, glossy, so there is a problem: for example, if one made a drawing on white rag paper, and if one varnishes it, it immediately becomes shiny, like the illustrations in popular women's magazines on glossy paper. There is no varnish that is totally matte. This problem took another six weeks to solve. Finally I found a young German artist living in New York, a very young man, whose speciality is varnishing large works for various artists. He has a high-pressure German spray-gun that makes a very fine mist. He came and put one coat of matte varnish on my black (because the blacks are the most susceptible to becoming glossy), two spray coats on the white, and then, by hand, put a third coat on the charcoal lines. (I had discovered that if I pressed the charcoal lines hard with my finger after the two previous varnishings, there were still charcoal bits crumbling underneath my finger.) With a "lining-brush," such as they use to stripe fine carriages and luxury automobiles, we all went over the major charcoal lines so they would really hold down. Theoretically for a very long time… but my greatest anxiety was to get a varnish that was not shiny. We came as close as is technically possible…

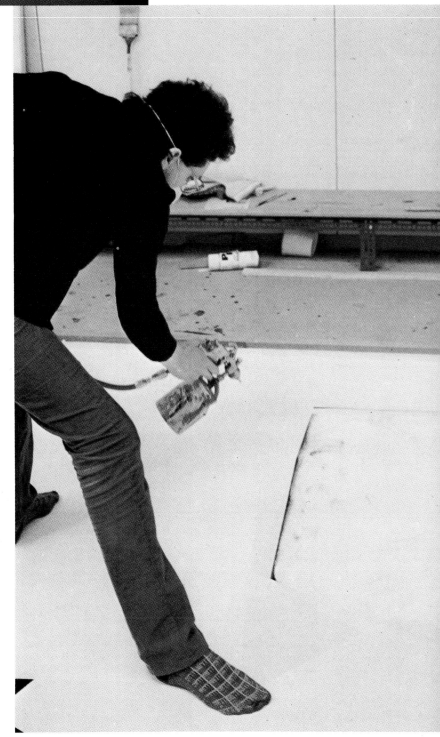

Two days later, LeBron Brothers, the art movers, came to pick up the mural, and to transport it to the National Gallery in Washington, D.C.

Bigelow and I laid a layer of "glassine" paper over the image, and rolled it onto a cardboard tube 24 inches in diameter. Then crated it, right there at the studio. We were anxious to get the thing stretched as soon as possible, so that there would be a minimal amount of abrasion or settling of the relatively recently sprayed varnish. At this point, the stretcher had already been fabricated, completely independently, and was being shipped down to Washington, D.C. Motherwell was ill, so Bigelow and I met the LeBron crew at the Museum in D.C.

Stretching the painting in Washington. ▶

LeBron fabricated a chassis that had a 3 inches wide edge, as opposed to the normal 2 inches. This stretcher was beefed up especially to accommodate this painting because of its large size. The LeBron fellows assembled the stretcher themselves, and had it raised off the ground about a meter or so, and at this point we very carefully unrolled the painting right onto the stretcher, which was elevated off the floor slightly more than one meter. Once the canvas was rolled out, Lenny and Charlie went to work stretching it; all Bigelow and I were really needed for was to make sure the canvas was stretched and attached in the right placement. We told Lenny and Charlie where we wanted it stretched, up to what edge, or line or mark on the canvas, according to Motherwell's instructions. We told them a centimeter or so deviation from the border line was as far as they could deviate, and, if we did have to deviate, we prefer to pretty much "center" the image, so we'd have an equal border. We didn't expect it to come really close to landing on the intended edge. As it worked out, it fit perfectly, within less than a sixteenth of one inch all the way around when it was stretched taut! So from all our calculation and planning, it came out to a sixteenth of an inch.

◀ *The painting is vertical for the first time.*

Reconciliation Elegy, *1978*.

Commission

E.A. CARMEAN, JR.

On June 1, 1978, the National Gallery of Art in America's Capital, Washington, D.C., opened its new East Building. A spectacular structure by the architect I.M. Pei, it exhibited that day seven specially commissioned works by Jean Arp, Alexander Calder, Anthony Caro, Joan Miró, Henry Moore, Robert Motherwell, and James Rosati. Each was of a large scale, scaled to the grand architecture. All of the works except the Caro and the Motherwell had been technically enlarged and fabricated at factories. Small maquettes were provided by each of the artists. But Caro constructed his sculpture and revised it at the site

◀ Interior views, East Building.

itself; and Motherwell's work – *the only painting* – had been made by himself in the artist's winter studios in Greenwich, Connecticut (30 miles from New York City). It would have perhaps been more convenient and certainly more practical to have had his work executed in a scenic-design factory studio in New York City, but he abhorred any sense of an enlarged replica. A radical change in size meant certain adjustments had to be made to keep a true sense of scale.

Pei's building is one of sharp geometric design. Based on an isosceles triangle, it centers on a skylit inner court 80 feet high, surrounded by galleries, balconies, and crossed by foot bridges.

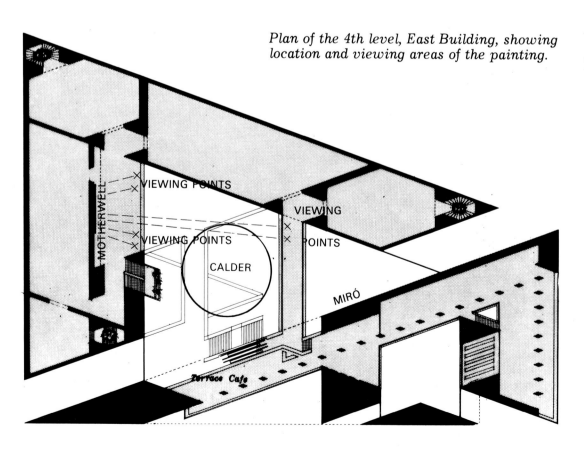

Plan of the 4th level, East Building, showing location and viewing areas of the painting.

LEVEL 4   MAIN GALLERY

Elegy to the Spanish Republic, No. 70, *1961*.

From the earliest preliminary plans, one wall in particular, of marble, was especially important. Part of the upper balcony, and visible across the great inner court, it too was skylit. The work of art on it would be the upper focal point of the East Building. Even more challenging, it would be seen under two different situations: part of this area is a normal gallery-sized space, and the painting (or mural) would be viewed in a large room-like setting; yet it would also be visible from a bridge 100 feet away, a bridge across and above the grand court, which has live trees planted in its marble floors, like an Italian village *piazza.*

In June, 1974, after six years of construction, the building had reached the stage where the Gallery could consider what should go on this marble wall. The consensus was to approach Robert Motherwell. Then fifty-nine years of age, Motherwell was the youngest of the American Abstract Expressionist generation. Since the flowering of that movement in New York in the 1940's, his art had continued to expand, and his perception, energy, and creativity had never been greater.

In October, 1974, I met with Motherwell, and introduced the proposed commission. From that moment on, he and I began to feel that the work should be the motif of the artist's *Elegy to the Spanish Republic* series. Begun in 1948, these works not only constituted one of his most profound motifs on living–and dying–but had also always been conceived as *public in tone,* in contrast to the more intimate expressions of his collages, drawings, and some of his other paintings. For the next two and one half years we studied together architectural plans and elevations, made various models, walked through the "under-construction" building, and talked repeatedly about the *Elegies.* In the Spring of 1977 Motherwell's concept of the painting-to-be emerged.

Conception

ROBERT MOTHERWELL

A critical artistic problem was my belief that, when a building is starkly "international style" in architecture, as is the Pei building, a painting in it also architectonic in character is hurt by the architecture. Geometrical painting is lost within massive simple architectural geometry, like a modernistic poster within an airport or railroad station. But what *can* compete in even greater architecture, such as, say, a Gothic cathedral, is *the human voice,* the human presence. I wanted a painting as clear and personal and unarchitectonic as a human voice, which is to say, a spontaneous work that sang, even though a solemn song... An elegiac tone... The voice of silence, even...

What I hoped to make then was on a 10 meter canvas to retain the immediacy of, say, oriental calligraphy in a work of huge enough scale (about

Study for Reconciliation Elegy.

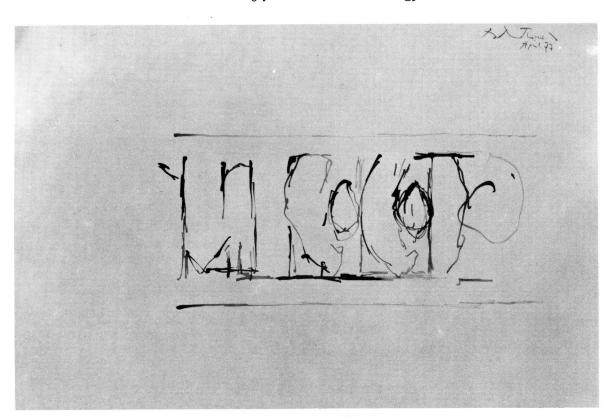

the same area as Picasso's *Guernica*), one that must hold, both *close-up, and from 100 feet away.* I myself never saw it from more than two meters, since it was painted on my studio floor: I had to guess at how the work would carry at 100 feet; and, because of illness at the time of installation, never even saw the painting *vertical,* hanging on a wall, until the night before the formal inaugural dinner, a dinner with speeches, and with music by Benny Goodman, my Connecticut neighbor, a favorite of Mr. Paul Mellon, the donor of the East Building, both more or less my contemporaries... as is I. M. Pei.

Problem: in the midst of architectural grandeur to strike a personal note, the note of the human presence... of a twentieth-century solitary individual, that terrible burden... and somehow make it public, too...

Ink sketch for Reconciliation Elegy.

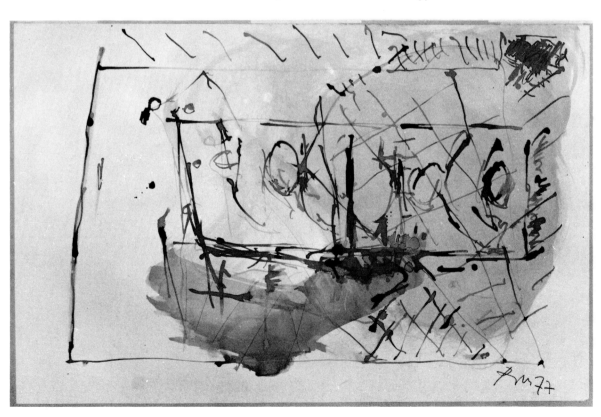

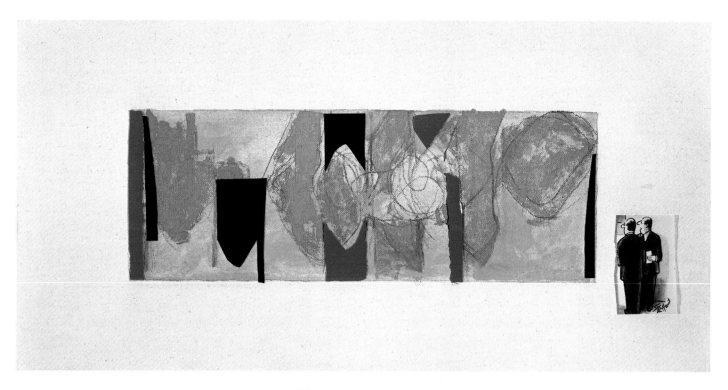

Elegy study, with collage.
A cartoon torn from The New Yorker *magazine gives the scale.*

E.A. CARMEAN, JR.

In April of 1977, Motherwell did two prospective sketches for the painting. Each in brown ink, done with a Japanese bamboo pen, they show the directness he was after. In August, I visited Motherwell at his summer studio in Provincetown, Cape Cod, Massachusetts. Three more drawings had been done. Very spare, in blue, his conception continued that the painting should be open and freely made, like an enormous sketch. In September, with nine months remaining before the scheduled opening, Motherwell sent to Washington the final two maquettes. Both were full painted sketches on canvas-board, the image about 16 inches wide. One, in brilliant blues and greens, also had collaged red and black papers, which the artist proposed to do in pasted canvas on the large painting. The other maquette was more dramatic, the image freely painted in black and white. After a period of discussion, Motherwell eliminated the color picture in favor of the black and white. The National Gallery agreed, and approved his commission. The painting would be 10 feet high and approximately 30 feet long, and at the Gallery's request, a large painting hung on the wall, *not* a mural.

ROBERT BIGELOW

Motherwell said at that time that, although the color maquette would be an interesting painting, nuanced brushed color was something he had never tried before on a huge scale, and he had no idea how it would come out, and he wasn't exactly sure how technically to approach it. And also we had the time schedule to think about. If the work wasn't successful, or if it didn't look like it was going "to make it"–we might not have had the time to start again.

I am attached to the same broad modernist tradition as Calder and Miró before me–strong, bright, intense, unmixed colors, contrasted with heavy black drawing–and I felt that my first, colored maquette conjoined with whatever Miró and Calder would do, would make too much a "period" ensemble… It would "date" *too* much, as Art Nouveau or Art Deco already have. My black and white maquette was more timeless as pure painting than my bright color and collage.

So I thought then, after much reflection… Twentieth-century modernism began optimistically, *à la* Apollinaire and Léger and Stravinsky, but after eighty years? What about Mandelstam and Kafka and Giacometti and Alban Berg and Black jazz?… Authoritarianism, bureaucracy, holocausts, nuclear terror, pollution, waste… Bright color no longer represents social reality but human aspirations… as in Gothic stained glass at the time of the Black Death.

Ink sketch for Reconciliation Elegy.

Preparation

ROBERT MOTHERWELL

I had tried about fifteen years earlier a large spontaneous wall painting (at the John F. Kennedy Federal Building in Boston, commissioned by Walter Gropius). I painted it on the "logical" premise (which turned out false) that the way one gains spontaneity is simply to paint spontaneously, as in sketching, regardless of physical size. But on a huge canvas when you are physically close to it in the act of painting, you can only see part of it; you don't know quite where physically you are: there is not sufficient peripheral vision... while in

Ink sketch from the Lyric Suite.

a small maquette, you see out of the corner of your eye, *all of it, all the time.* Instinct places everything justly... Having failed to satisfy myself with the Kennedy mural in retrospect, I thought I must proceed otherwise... to use every technical resource at my command to give spontaneity, that is, the *illusion* that the work was both conceived (which it was) and executed (which it nearly was) with total immediacy in one energetic day.

E.A. CARMEAN, JR.

New England Elegy, 1966, had been commissioned by the United States Government for a new Walter Gropius building with 30,000 office workers in Government Center in Boston. Motherwell had wanted to make a very active, freely painted image, to stand out against the rigid modular structure of the architecture. Months earlier, he was working on a set of 1000 small ink paintings on rice paper, using the technique of "automatism"—no conscious preconceptions and no revisions. Nearly six hundred were made before the series was interrupted when Motherwell's close friend sculptor David Smith was killed in a

New England Elegy *installed in the*
John F. Kennedy Building, Boston, Massachusetts.

truck accident. The next year, Motherwell at-
tempted the idea of "automatism" with simple
forms in the Kennedy mural, even at its scale of
10 x 15 feet. (In making the *New England Elegy*,
a certain association may have been in the artist's
mind between the brutal, bloody death of an
American President from Massachusetts and
that of David Smith in Vermont, both states con-
tiguous in the New England region of the United
States, where Motherwell lives.)

73

Conclusion

ROBERT MOTHERWELL

White has always conveyed to me the radiance of life, so that if one—though this is too literal—if one takes the *Elegies* as a metaphor for "life and death," then obviously a sense of life as freedom and of death as the terminal vivifier, can be an endless obsession and preoccupation. In a curious way in the *Reconciliation Elegy* my black forms, the life-death forms, are becoming personages, instead of black stones… the black and white are beginning to merge… In 1974, I had five major surgical operations during three weeks, and "died" twice on the operating table. As a youth, I had asthma, as badly as Proust, and often was literally choking to death, if I didn't get an injection of adrenalin in time. Death has been a continual living presence to me, so to speak. I perhaps generalized it, as artists do, into something less personal, through various devices, titles, generalized forms, certain plastic weights, through events whose death I deeply cared about, that of the Spanish Republic, that of my friend David Smith the sculptor, and so on…

What modern persons have in common is the "subjective," the domains of feeling, more so than conscious idealogies. When I know of persons their religion, their race, their politics, and their other ideas, these to me are less fundamentally revealing than when they express (often indirectly) their subjective feelings. Emotions undercut superimposed idealogies. In one sense, the

effort of modern art is to express the universality of the "subjective" through a visual "object"… for another person to share… the perception and the discrimination… To experience radiance, the emotion that radiates from the "object"… The ecstatic has various modes and tones, in art as in life. If the object is an artifact, *merely* an "object," an *objet d'art,* the "subjective" ecstasy is diminished. The experience of ecstasy distinguishes us from both animals and "objects," and is one of the profoundest human needs, a need so deep a person will do irrational or self-destructive acts to satisfy it, rather than live as an "object" in a social scheme. Spontaneity and ecstasy are entangled, and both have as final enemies authoritarianism and death.

At Five in the Afternoon, *1949.*

Reconciliation

ROBERT MOTHERWELL

The function of my titles is partly negative, to mark off what *can't be named* in the picture. (The cubists were positively literal in their titles—Picasso calls a painting of an apple and a pipe, no matter how abstract, "Apple and Pipe." My work is not literal in the cubist sense.) The Washington painting was entitled *Reconciliation Elegy* for several reasons. Partly from a conversation the same year with the Spanish artist Tápies *chez moi* about the new hopes for humanism in Spain— my *Elegies to the Spanish Republic* had been meant, on one level, as an elegy for the tragically missed opportunity of Spain to enter the liberal modern world in the 1930's. And for its tragic suffering then and for decades after. The title must also unconsciously correspond to a certain subjective stage in my own life. Life and death are now to me subjectively less antagonistic—less sharply opposed: to put it the other way around, both are absorbed by the natural process of living. Apollinaire once wrote that "Crowds rush toward death": but I see with age that death is part of life, not the opposite. Thus *Reconciliation* has multiple meanings... *Reconciliation* (hopefully) of the Spanish peoples, reconciliation with Death and Life... Against the background of possible nuclear holocaust, we must even reconcile ourselves to the fact that western man, in choosing centuries ago to exploit nature rather than marry her, has doomed himself... with an industrial technology for which there is neither the wisdom nor the political mechanism to control... The *Reconciliation Elegy* is not less for Spain, but is also for all mankind... Meanwhile, each individual seeks his own private ecstasy...

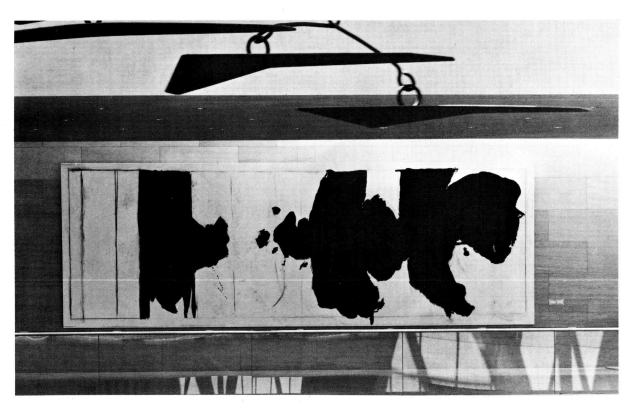

Reconciliation Elegy *seen from the bridge.*

Acrylic paint on photograph, study for revision A.

Study for revision B.

78

Revision

E.A. CARMEAN, JR.

ROBERT MOTHERWELL

Reconciliation Elegy was hung in the East Building on March 22, 1978. Motherwell was briefly ill that spring, and thus didn't see it up on the wall until the evening before the building opened to the public on June 1. Within the space in front of the picture it has a sonority and richness that is new to the *Elegy* series. But from the bridge 100 meters away Motherwell felt that perhaps the image was too spare, or that the border around the image gave it too much white, diluted its intensity. The National Gallery's position was – as it had been during the conception and in the commission contract – that the final "approval" on the painting in that space was given to the artist.

Beginning August 1979, Motherwell made studies for revising the picture.

Perhaps after all the *Elegy* image motif needs to be more monumental (sculptural) against the hard Pei architecture. Because I tried to make a spontaneous sketch, my work in Washington does have an energetic impulse that it might not otherwise. If I were to revise it, making it more monumental, it may still retain its liveliness, a dancing quality, of forms dancing quite different in tone from the tomb-like, ritualistic, atavistic forms of the principal early *Elegies*. Who knows? Nowadays the artist is brought into the architectural project too late in the process. If I had had the whole wall... A mural is required here, not a separate painting, no matter how large, hung on a marble wall...

Perhaps the sheer technological complexity of a massive modern building's actual construction does not pause long enough to allow the human voice to "feel" its way in, to sense and revise and refine until the exactly appropriate tone of voice is found... No matter how handsomely an artist is paid, his payment is nothing compared to the financial cost of halting construction work and hundreds of workers for breathing time, to make adjustments that can only be made through emotion, since a certain emotion is ironically (and especially with an art museum) the whole point of the building. Otherwise simply make a climatically controlled mausoleum, for the physical preservation of "objects"...

Or the actual painting should *not* be able to be seen from such a great distance, but closed in, to reflect the intimacy of the conditions under which it was created in the studio. It is alive close up, the situation of its creation...

◀ *Robert Motherwell in Greenwich, 1979.*

Chronology

1974 November 22	E. A. Carmean, Jr., visits Robert Motherwell in Greenwich, Connecticut, to discuss the possibility of a commissioned painting for the National Gallery's East Building. Subsequently, architectural plans and photographs are sent to Greenwich.
1975 April 27	After discussing the project during the winter, Motherwell and Carmean meet again in Greenwich, with more detailed plans of the upper level area. It is agreed at this meeting the work should be in the artist's *Elegy to the Spanish Republic* series.
May 1	A scale replica of the artist's largest *Elegy* to date, *No. 100*, 1965, is put into position in an architectural model of the East Building.
August 31	In his summer studio in Provincetown, Massachusetts, Motherwell paints *Spanish Death,* extrapolating the image from an earlier *Elegy,* No. 70.
October 15	Carmean visits Motherwell in Greenwich with more detailed plans and elevations. At this time they discuss *Elegy No. 100,* which has been brought into the studio for revision.
November 10	Motherwell pays his first visit to the National Gallery to study the architectural model and the rough construction of the upper level of the East Building.

November 12

Motherwell completely revises *Elegy No. 100*, with more massive and architectural forms on the right, and the *Spanish Death* motive on the left. A scale replica of this revised painting is now put into the East Building model.

Elegy to the Spanish Republic, No. 100 *(revised), 1963-1975.*

1976
February 4

J. Carter Brown, Director, and Paul Mellon, President of the National Gallery, review the proposed Motherwell commission and study various maquettes in the East Building. They are enthusiastic about the concept and give full approval for the project to continue.

March 23

Carmean flies to Boston to study *New England Elegy*, the artist's largest commissioned painting, at the John F. Kennedy Federal Building, in Government Center.

Installation view, The Subjects of the Artist, *National Gallery of Art, Washington, 1978.*

March 24	Carmean visits Motherwell in Greenwich. They discuss the relative failure of the Boston mural. At this same meeting, while discussing the evolution of the *Elegies* for the National Gallery exhibition, *Subjects of the Artist,* Motherwell makes a doodle to illustrate the origin of the original image. This is the first time since the creation of the image that Motherwell has revealed this process. "Automatism" behind the theme becomes of crucial importance, and now the question of spontaneity–at a large scale–is seen as the central issue in the large commission picture.

Two ink sketches, 1976.

October 7	Carmean and Motherwell meet in Greenwich to discuss the project further.
November 30	Motherwell visits Washington to see the East Building, where construction has advanced to the stage where the basic forms of the upper level space are completed. He studies the model and requests a similar scale maquette be prepared for the Greenwich studio. Samples of the grey-pink wall marble are also sent.

1977
April

Motherwell makes several brown ink sketches for the project.

May 2

Two brown ink sketches proposed by the artist arrive in Washington. Using these, a third scale maquette is placed in the model, and photographs showing this are sent to Provincetown.

Third revised maquette in scale model of East Building, May 1977.

July 6

As the Motherwell painting will be under a skylight, tests are made to determine the path of sunlight over the work during the day, and to study how a partial screening device can be installed.

August 1-15

For two intensive weeks Carmean and Motherwell discuss the *Elegies,* for the *Subjects of the Artist* exhibition. Three more drawings are made for the project.

September

Motherwell makes two final maquettes for the project, one in color with collaged panels to be duplicated in collaged canvas; the other in black and white. The choice is left to the Board of Trustees of the National Gallery, and at their September 25 meeting they approve the color *Elegy.*

October 8

Motherwell and Carmean meet in Greenwich, where the 4 × 12 meter canvas is being stretched on the studio floor. They discuss the technical difficulties of the color *Elegy.*

November 18

In a long telephone conversation, Motherwell outlines to Carmean why the color *Elegy* is not appropriate for the East Building. He subsequently writes to Director Brown and requests that the black and white maquette be approved. At the same time studio assistants John Scofield and Robert Bigelow continue applying three coats of gesso to the canvas.

December	Using a 4 × 8 feet photographic enlargement, Bigelow and Scofield make a paper cartoon 12 × 40 feet, matching the size of the painting. At their December meeting the Gallery's Board of Trustees approves the black and white maquette.
1978 January 25	Bigelow and Scofield transfer the cartoon image to the canvas by pricking the paper and pouncing red chalk through the holes.
January 28	Carmean visits Greenwich and sees the chalk sinopia image on the canvas.
January 30–February 14	Motherwell paints *Reconciliation Elegy*.
February 22	Carmean sees the painting still on the studio floor in Greenwich, and discusses with Motherwell the problem of varnishing the picture.
March 3	With the painting still placed unprotected on the studio floor, Motherwell and Carmean discuss spraying the picture with a light varnish.
March 8	*Reconciliation Elegy* is varnished.
March 22	*Reconciliation Elegy* arrives rolled at the East Building and is installed, after stretching.
June 1	The East Building opens to the public. The evening before, Motherwell sees the painting vertical for the first time, and in place.

E. A. Carmean, Jr. on the fourth level bridge.

1979
January 1

Carmean and Motherwell meet in Greenwich to discuss the painting. Motherwell expresses his concern about the strength of the work, in reference to the pictorial space around the image and the quantity of empty space on the left side.

June 15

In a telephone conversation, Motherwell and Carmean again discuss the work, and Motherwell inquires about making changes. The Gallery confirms the decision rests with the artist.

August 2–18

Carmean and Motherwell meet in Provincetown to further discuss revisions. Working on photographs of the painting, Motherwell begins making maquettes of possible changes. He is deeply moved by the openness and faith of the National Gallery.

BOOK DESIGN BY LAURO VENTURI
FILMSET BY TYPELEC, GENEVA
ILLUSTRATIONS BY LITH-ART, BERN
PRINTED BY IMPRIMERIES RÉUNIES, LAUSANNE

PHOTOGRAPHIC CREDITS

Robert Bigelow: p. 10 right, 17 bottom, 18, 21, 23, 24, 25, 26, 27, 28, 29, 30, 31, 32, 34, 35, 36, 37, 38, 39, 40, 41, 42, 43, 44, 45, 46, 47, 49, 50, 51, 53, 56 bottom, 58, 59 top, bottom right, 60; Dennis Brack, Black Star: p. 6; Richard Fallon: p. 73; Betty Fiske: p. 10 top, 13, 16; Peter A. Juley: p. 76; Renate Ponsold: p. 9, 22, 80; John E. Scofield: p. 10 bottom, 12, 17 top, 19, 33, 55, 56 top, 57, 59 center, bottom left; Steve Sloman: 2-3, 81, 82; National Gallery of Art, Washington D.C.: p. 14, 62-63, 64, 65, 74-75, 78 top, 82 top, 83; The Metropolitan Museum of Art, New York: p. 66; M. Knoedler and Co., Inc.: p. 15; provided by the Artist: p. 68, 69, 70, 72.

The original edition of

Reconciliation Elegy

includes 75 copies numbered from 1 to 75
and 15 copies *Hors Commerce* numbered
h.c. 1 to h.c. 15.
Each of those 90 copies is accompanied
by an original lithograph by Robert Motherwell
signed and numbered by the artist.

PUBLISHED AUGUST 1980

PRINTED IN SWITZERLAND